FULL MOON

SILVER GLIMPSES

Poetry & Prose

by

Gloria Jewel Leitner

Gloria Jewel Leitner

Little Wing Publishing   San Francisco, Ca.

Also by the author:

Poems of Song & Passion (1975)

Lovebud: Expectations of the Heart (1978)

Photo on back cover by Alan Steinheimer.

Many thanks to Ellie Heymann and Caryn Sherne.

ISBN 0-9617633-1-0

CONTENTS

And so the dance begins —

my heart leaps!

The Seeking

Laughter is the intention
Of the right way of living --
Amber, silver, effervescent songs.

I reach into the night
For his words, scent, smile,
Look for the sapphires of love
To shower like spring raindrops . . . .
Hope for the long, arching wave
To come and sweep me,
Arms wide like wings,
To the pearl-bright shore.

Midnight blue,
The shine upon my ringed finger;
Castles built by thoughts,
Their spires pointing moonward --
O ancient sphinx,
Who spins the Wheel of Fortune!
Are you waiting for my yearning to melt
Into a calm, clear pool of patience,
For my heart to learn
Its slow, bittersweet message,
Before you bring the flowerlight of my life
From out of the shadows
To my eye's dawn?

The Gardener

I cannot push the future:
I can only spread the seeds,
And carefully tend the soil --
For the seasons start and end
Of their own accord.

And a harvest before the time is ripe
Will yield a few small fruit;
But a hurried crop will satiate
Neither the palate, nor the soul.

Another Way

The freedom to live is no hallucination:
   a rose breaks the concrete monotony,
   a sunbeam shafts through leaden air,
   a golden glimpse
   unlocks the mind's dark coffins.

For the soaring eagle signals
   our privilege to Be;
The sparkling flame of moon-wave
   marks a promise.

And vibrance is a gown of skin,
   intimate with peace:
   the poise of perfection.

The Challenge

But if one is not delighted
    with the course
    of one's life,

Why not chance
    the risk
    of change?

An Art & A Balance

Life
    is anything but simple.
The sureties play us for fools,
    take us for a ride
    then leave us stranded --
The things that seem indubitable,
    indubitably
        are not.

How to walk that tightrope line
    and not to shudder;
How to laugh & love,
    still ready for the fall;
How to beat the drum,
    but be fully aware of the silence;

How to kiss good-bye
    what you care for most of all.

A Lesson in Definition

Certainly a log --
    cedar, pine, what-have-you --
Can serve as a seat as well as an armchair,
    upholstered & fancy-footed.

The moral of the story:

Form is fact,
But creativity is using
    what others may not believe.

A Knowledge, A Wisdom

I cleared my eyes,
 and polished my memory --
  ebony reflected my mood
  much more than gold.
A deep reflective wonder
 coaled my soul like a raven's wing,
  like a cove-dark sea,
   canoed,
   oars dipping,
Thru a quiet, solemn-sweet eve
 where silence rings.

Enchantment does not always blaze
 with razzle-dazzle ways --
The way of muted riches
 hums a deeper tone,
  like a satin drum
  or a dew-fall.

And the lulling current cures, calms,
 negates mundane pursuits --
Leaving only the essence:
 primordial seeds
 of a soft, original dawning.

The Treasure

A red velvet brocade encircled her heart,
A green, lemony-green veil draped her eyes.
And inside her mind dwelt a crystal
Of milky white.

These, the riches betrothed,
These, the gems endowed.

And to request more,
To seek additional coins of another realm --

Seemed as silly as a queen
Desiring to wear a second crown.

The School

The lessons culled from life are silent --
We absorb a certain serenity of motion,
   a knowledge --
Or rather, an intuitive sense
   of how to coincide, absolutely,
     with the perfect path for our selves.

The path is not one that can be
   pointed out by another,
Or delineated in books,
   or dreamt ahead of its time.

It is a path that unwinds as we walk,
   that shows as we approach,
That leads without signs
   deciphered by the mind.

To learn to harmonize with that path
   is to learn to be one with all that it crosses --
To experience obstacles as aids,
   enriching every twisting turn & step.

A student of the stillness
   can sing or shout or cry,
Discourse at length,
   or whisper to the stars.
But at all times, and in all ways,
   the rippled flow resides inside:
The conquest is proven
   in the clearness of your eyes.

The Philosopher's Question

Do we take our values
And deify them?
Our cherished ideals
And reify them?
What our idols speak
Our hearts cannot deny.

For what is truer,
A bowl of rice --
Or a god?

World Without God

Divinity
    scissor-scrapped
    by shears of sharp-edged
    ignorance

The jealousies
    like armor
    hide the tender
    heart's reply

The jittle-clank
    of tin & discord
    overlay
    the harp-chords

And the people
    do not hear
    the angels cry.

Nightshow

In blackness among
The clustered stars,
Omen
Token
Opal
Hymn
Paler than an orange glass marble:
Full lunar eclipse
In the warm night hills.

Okeover

Shreds of mist
Hung like a shawl,
Like a soft cape,
A silent scarf
On shoulders of hills
That layered the forest inlet

As our kayak skimmed so smoothly,
Sliced the water's hush
Almost ripple-less,
We could have been seal or salmon,
Shark or dolphin.

As we slid up the coast
Of wild-quiet beauty,
Slid by mossy greens,
Slid past rocky cliffs
With branching arms
Arbutus red . . . .

Slid under clouds,
Over seas,
Through the air:
A softly
   rolling
      pearl.

November

Liquid forest,
    raindropped clean --
I am unmasked in your naked branches,
Taken to luminous realms
    by lime-bright moss
    and glossy, wet-lick leaves.

And the ferns wear a necklace
    of waterbead silver,
And the showers gem-drop the trees,
And the shoots of new grass,
    in a cradle of black,
    bathe away,
    a cascade of green.

Yes, the Oregon fall means renewal,
    dust rinsed from summer trees,
Drinking the free-flowing wine that pours
    from a cloud-laden, generous heaven --
And the forest, exuberant, shines
    like a swift-rushing stream.

Tale of the Seasons

Lord of Winter Wisdom, Lord of White:
    your lessons are patient, silent waiting,
    gathering together,
    enduring.

Lord of Spring Emergence, Lord of Green:
    your lessons are newness and revival,
    bloom and smiling eyes,
    giving.

Lord of Summer Favor, Lord of Gold:
    your lessons are passion, light and fire,
    brilliance with no bounds,
    out-going.

Lord of Autumn Caring, Lord of Red:
    your lessons are cooling, fresh and swift,
    the harvest taking in,
    saying good-bye.

Living Naturally

A home of leaved canopy and mossy carpet,
Wall-hangings of berried vines,
Flowerbells and seats of ancient stumps,
And the river my radio;

Decor every rich and brilliant green & gold & brown,
Dimensions unlimited,
Roommates beyond number --
Birds, insects, animals, trees;

No rent, no payments to the landlord above:
Just the paying of attention,
The dues of a grateful heart.

She Comes

Bronze sound of cymbals,
     trilling tambourines,
          flute and avocado-rich song --

The vocalization of Dawn,
     emerald-eyed and rosy-lipped
          upon the mountain.

Judge Not the Source

The rain showered down like a mother
   embracing her child --
Unrestrained,
     the fullest giving of sky-water
       to earth & rock,
        tree, leaf & flower.

The greens gleamed, the yellows glowed --
   a world of vibrant color
     beneath a hood of ancient gray.

Thus Beauty and Good sometimes spring forth
   from dark and somber places --

As light is a brilliant fire that bursts
   from the darkest brown of wood.

Malaspina Farm

The peace rested upon the night
   like a filament of silver;
An ebony sky held the moon-brightened clouds
   in its dark and sweetened cup.
And the cabin held the three --
   Tony, Margaret, Gloria;
Though one was not yet sleeping.

By the golden light of a kerosene lamp,
   cuddled in covers, she wrote;
Listened to creeks in the forest night,
   the flit of a moth against ceiling;
Watched liquidly still the gleaming brass,
   the satiny red-blonde cedar;
The glassy reflection
   of a wide-eyed, dark-haired lady (herself)
   in the window.

Breeze rustled trees,
   a pink rose bowed its head,
   surrounded by green;
The stream of sound-within-no-sound sang
   with a voice like a long, thin bell.

By and by, Time gently closed the lids
   of her weighty eyes;
And sliding down, she silently spoke
   the ending words of day:
Good-night to the world,
Hello to the sleeping dreamer.

Rima

On the incessant whispers of forest breathing,
  like foam upon the moving waters,
Her voice rides.
The lilts coincide, the rhythms dance,
  old partners.

Born of nature's stock,
Bred by the rules of the green,
Built by the suns of time
  and the reeds of passage --

She does not know bird as bird,
  but as the part of her that flies;
Not sky as what's above,
  but the high, blue skin that visits day.

Walking on the earth,
  brown-toed in the brown rich soil;
Arms that graze companions' leafy arms --
She is formed by the stroke of an artist
  beyond brush, beyond palette --
Colors adorning her hair,
The landscape her aura.

Embankments of lakes, pools and ponds
    are fringed with her forest of scent;
The fields and mountain flanks
    are rendered fertile by her smile.

And in all of this abundance,
    this treasure transcending coin
    or computation --
A queen in nature's kingdom,
    who could ask for anything more?

Beginning

Pink/gray cloud-rise morning,
Bluejay echoes, meadows,
Sun is ripe and casting forth
Her golden star-winged angels,
Cherishing life's movements
And the fondling
Of her babes.

Evolution

The tide glows;
    the moon-lighted paths
    undulate, roll,
    bob up and down
    with winds, rhapsodic tempos . . . .

While the living beings of the liquid womb,
    feeling the magic above,
Mix with the bubbles of crystal blue,
    and laugh with the weaving seaweed
    of green and maroon.

And here upon the face of the world,
    in our womb of earth and sky,
We, too, feel the pull of what's high above:
    the stars that speak
    with the night.

And we grow, because we need to;
And we heed the realer signs;
And we slip into the vine-filled cavern
    where the reds are warm,
    the air a furry cape,
    the seasons fresh
    with winter's time to bide . . . .
Then emerge from our place
    to the gleam-vision night:
    to stretch our minds
    like petaled wings of light.

Autumn

Gingerly, I stepped about the leaf:
Brown as cinnamon,
   crisp-crinkled at my feet,
It presaged fall;
Cool;
Ravens over the sharp gray winter sea;
Mountains with snow-flowing rivers
   resounding down green-thighed flanks,
      a sparkling . . . .

And then the limbs, bare, upreaching,
   swept my eye, chin,
Lifted my spirit to a strength beyond reason;
A beauty raw yet polished,
   and unimpeachable
      as only nature can be.

The visions were like visitors
   on pot-of-tea days,
When the fire crackles
   and the frost pearls the afternoon sky;
When early sunsets and the strange mystique
   of a silent, cold-licked dawn
      hold my breath like a crystal.

I inhaled with a depth
   unknown in the season of constant warmth,
Cheeks flushed with vigorous walking.

When I heard the birds,
   I marveled --
Not like the sweet lyrical spirits of spring
   (calls of a softly golden timing) --

These warbles charmed
   by their startling clarity,
A blade of sound
   piercing the air
      like a C-sharp bell of glass --
         cold-bright
      like a winter star.

Beyond Grasp, Beyond Measure

Experience defies defining,
    divining --
Surprising is nature's way of showing,
    not to tell.

Using The Rational Mind

Causes:
    how to discern
    without destroying
    the bigger picture.

Courses:
    how to follow
    without losing sight
    of the source, the shore.

Rollering the Coaster

The time of laughter,
Like the time of labor and pain,
Must have its day.

And all the chortles in our belly,
The chuckles in our brain,
The giggles and the wriggles
And the tickle-silly grins

Serve to cushion us
Against the next great fall.

Lovesphere

The realm of the heart's dedication --
    soul to soul,
    body to flesh,
    lips to kissing comprehension.

Dynamism whose energy is ebbless --
    all the elements, ecstacies, enticements,
    on a wind of vividness,
        a wind of elated wings:
Potion
    of a high-water mark heart.

Love is anguish turned upside-down,
    anger inside-out;
Love is depression
    doing a head-stand.

And in that shining circle,
    every line and angle meets:
        corners curve and sharpness rounds
        like soft and kittenish eyes.

Mazurka

The variance dance
In threadbare dress,
Dripping from the rain

Or cozy in a coat of fur,
Protected from the pain --

Sun shines,
    and I dance;
Moon shines,
    what else can I do?
Soul shines:
    my heart dances out the door.

An Eloquent Mime

Molten in the sky
    of love's horizon,

Lip-moves,
    wordless speech
        of languorous eyes.

The Signet

Because of you
    I wear
        the gypsy-ring of fortune.

You

Lately
    all the infinites have sought one corner,
        one purpose,
        one face;
All the verities coalesced
    to a syllable.

And the pearl has the rays
    of every shining;
The laughter,
    the ring
        of every human-to-human smile.

Companion

The spray of the fountain threw its flowers out, wide-spiraling past my nostrils . . . hair . . . wind on my eyelashes gentle. The scent and the sound like wine singing crystal arias to long-stemmed glasses; the cupping yet formless mood, as though an inexplicable force, unchained and unfolding, constantly renewing, surrounded -- with warmth and security in its very freedom of unbounded, far-flung wandering . . . . Like the forest -- trees of the wilderness as mothering and ordered as Nature the comforter herself.

The tales of ancient women filled my head, and the throaty whispers of falling night, brooks and rivers running. I ascended the stony hillock, and took assessment. It all stood, splendored and untouched -- the moonlight a sharp, cold-sweet edging to the landscape below. The cliff was by all reasoning the highest apex of this corner of the world; yet it seemed dwarfed, outdone by the peaks and points in the distance, rock-hard and gliding forever upward.

When I listened, I noted neither birds chirping nor any distinct animal sound -- but a mesh of humming and blue/green, life process noises. Softly I stroked his hair -- in my mind, he was forever with me. We lived in eternal silence and internal conversation, always and yet never together. . . . We were like beads on an abacus, moved back and forth by the hand of fate, in some transcendent form of calculation: for what sum, we did not know. But here we were, unified no matter whither we had been tossed by the fickle finger.

We were not stranded -- no, lost was the wrong word. We were neither too weak to admit it, nor too blinded to the facts we faced. Rather, it was as though the sweeping wind that rocked us from there to here, and here to who-can-tell, was our friend -- an acquaintance we did not know intimately, but trusted nevertheless. This being without foundation, flying on routeless wing, rotation by way of a pivot neither seen nor heard -- was as reassuring as a bed when a child and the sandman filled our eyes, and the arms of mama divined so. We were placed in a cozy-doze spot, patted, gentled, and told to dream -- freely.

How could we do anything else but follow?

And did I seem indifferent to the plague raining around me? I hope not -- for it was not as I felt. My heart still bled, tears cried, fingers easily grasped for the line: to tie up the evil for good, to throw it away. But yet, Time taught me much more patience . . . for I could do only as circumstances and spirit enabled.

And so I sharpened my eyes by the light of inward sight, and kept myself strong for the chance. Grace, and justice; courage, and forgiveness; eager to live, and to give. These were the notions for which we aimed, as two -- as one.

"Sing!" he commanded. I obeyed, and gave

him a melody of richness and petals. I could feel his heartbeat, faster now by the smiling tempo I sang him. It was as though this tie, like an umbilical cord that nurtured (yet who was the mother, and who the babe?) — this connection gave access to the cellular secrets that lay inside our breasts. We walked on a path that climbed and tunneled, circled and slipped, shot up again and then under, and still we ended, and began again, as a whole.

The ship of air took us to stellar conjectures; the wooded river gave us dark, glossy feelings to sail upon through the drifting of night. And in the days of living, here and there a sun peeped out, shining on the backs and topmost heads of clouds like a scattering of sand-jewels flung across the sky. The gold-beige grains lit the tufting masses, and these lit our eyes. Even when we shut our lids like a curtain, we could see — with a vividness that at times surpassed the pictures outside our mind.

How could we exist without this dialogue, this understanding, this fortunate, breathing contact? We were one with another, and in one another; we knew very little, but that we would survive. Indelibly, the lesson was impressed (our blood was thicker for it) — and the lesson was what we became (our thoughts were richer for it) — and the lesson chose us, and we it, like a prince and a princess.

Midnight Rider

Violet is the night --
　　　violet and crested.

As crescent sweeps of waves
　　　caress the beach
　　　with white-winged froth,

I toss my mane:
　　　ready for the moon-timed gallop.

Love Is a Centering

The textual, audio-visual reality of a sensate world,
    as clearly, cleanly, crisply resolved
        as by the lens of a green-glass wing
            of a soaring eagle.

The shot-thru-with-vividness crunch
    of this sweet, brilliant red apple --
Like the memory of his lips,
    every line in them irresistible:
        the full-blooded, almost violet tinge
        to his luscious, laughing-curved mouth
        that plays
        like his crystal-ball blue eyes.

Crickets accenting the night's focused silence,
    while Venus, like a golden fireball,
        hangs her torch between the stars . . . .
The pink scrolled lamp,
    glass artfully cracked
        like a shattered sheet of ice . . . .
While I, chin in hands, green-sweater soft,
    stroke the pencil to a page.

Chinese bells out the window,
    neighbors and bark of dogs,
Nobody in the room or house --
    but she who dwells at base, at root
        of the heart.

Emancipation

Bought -- the lavenders have sold me,
        soul and all,
            to the whim of the heavens.

Bought -- shorn clean of habits,
        roots,
            the ancient fears of pain.

No longer free to act unfree,
I've been bought -- and sold -- out of slavery:

Lord, what cosmic knavery!

The Quest

Many expressions of the turquoise hue:
    jingling my bells,
    stringing up crystals and bells to feathers,
       I play the opal flute.

Out from the depths of my reaches,
    the realm where the wind meets the sun,
    and the pond, the moist of the soil:
So much passion, so much toil,
    so much thinking in lofty phrases, praises,
    dawnlight hazes,
       sainted & scented birth as jasmine white.

Meditating in the morning on the light,
    feeling an archway of lit-up thoughts and dreams,
       and sailing yonder.

Hope upon hope, watching for the glisten
    of a passerby --
       to catch his eye,
       to love another.

Who understands with my perception,
    games through life with prayer
    (and sometimes tears) --
And all because you want it so badly,
    the heights of spirited splendor.

It is only a life-cloth that I sew, hem, mend
   out of cotton and velvet;
Only a time-line of giving, of knowing,
   of watching the petals come alive,
      and fall;
Only a single, a simple, a sole soul surviving,
   as I can
      in a boat
         rushing waters,
         the waves & the winters,
         the waiting & dreams.

Yet here, here I am,
   safe and not lonely,
   in essence a pearl in the shell of a lamb.

Holy as a walnut brown, a leaf,
   a surf of twilight green
      dipped in moongold --
Over the weeds of past-time sorrows,
   the seeds of inner remorse,
I am riding a horse of a shimmering color:
   oh, lover I sing in the pine-meadow trees.

As it happens,
   day by day,
   the baking of cakes in the wood-burning oven,
   cinnamoned raisins
      and aromas forthwith

Rows of corn, of teeth, of ages,
   hues of settling sun,
   the run of a thunderroll over the earth.

Back, back in the ferned and weathered wood,
   the visions and moanings of rivers;
   the curtain of leaves, the instant of showers,
      the diamond-eye glimpses of "I".

Only in tallest field-flowers,
   and blue as eyes,
   and ruby gems, the blossoms at the bottom
      of the towering fir . . . .
In liquid, motioned air,
   red-dirted paths thru hills unwinding.

Aura of justness,
   of pebbles of every color in the creek,
Aura of hinted daybreak,
   and sacred, sharp-as-sword night,
      and stabbing stars.

Morning pictures of snow-packed mountains:
   majestic under sun, passive under gray --
      thus they appear.
And these I wear as an earring of emerald dangles.

Unforsaken,
    encircled by bodies, eyes,
    glasses of milkshake smiles --
Towers built of flowers' graceful lines,

Then coming to rest
    at the berrybush hedge
    of sweet-juice, tonguing succulence;

Coming to test my powers
    of patience,
    selfless strength;

All in the length of hours
    I sit and ponder,
    walk and stretch my muscles,

Seek for the sky:
    the hour's finding.

Fingers in the Pie: Oh, My!

Life won't be second-guessed,
Or talked to like a foreign guest.

Jump <u>in</u> --
To the heart of the action!

Inside Passage

Time, said Einstein,
Is relative.

Indeed --
One doesn't have to approach
   the speed of light,
Compare the voyager's watch
   with the observer's,
To draw this rule.

Elongation comes with pointed awareness,
Being pivoted at the crux.
This, the personal verification,
The irrefutable proof.

The stretching out of time
Beyond the pace of clock-face numbers,
Creating enormous space
   in which a thousand moments,
   or the single deepest insight,
Can occur in the tick of a tock --

No calculus can ever subtract
   from what occurs inside the soul;
No physicist add to what's written
   in the sacred book of life.

The Harvest

How is it that the unknown comes to blossom?

The seeds are sometimes so well hidden
    we do not even know they've been planted,
    and who has watered,
    and cared for them.

Yet the fruits that come as a surprise are sweeter,
    by far,
    than what we consciously cultivate --

For it is the crop that's nurtured
    by the hidden streams of life,
    the hidden light of suns beyond the stars --

That gleams with jewel-ripe shine
    and leads Beyond.

The Connector

How liberating it is
    to give up one's expectations!

For then the disappointment disappears;
The future's left on its own,
    in its raw, awesomely uncircumscribed state --
With every possibility for ill
    as likely as every one for good.

And with a strand of hope
    as thick as a jungle vine
        that swings astonishingly
            between skyscraping palms and fronds,

That carries one across the jaws
    of a crocodile-laden lagoon --

With that unbreakable rope of faith to hold on to,
    you'll always make it,
    whole,
        to the other side.

Awash

Blue is the shimmer of the sea
As it rolls my way.

And I am tempted to loll,
   like a baby in its first bath,
      to sink beneath the liquid,
     let it lap upon my face,
       cape me and cap me,
       anoint and cleanse,
        like a friend.

For the waters hold life --
   like a glove, like a chalice,
     receptor/protector
     of all living things.

The Egret

Sunlight glinting on mudflats,
   and the palm trees' silence,
      agreeing . . . .
A late afternoon, warm-brown, quiet,
   end-of-day sort of feeling . . . .

Reflections of a watercolor sky:
   in its midst, an egret lands --
A simple, smooth, bone-clean declination:
   beak long,
      body lean,
         sleek-sailing . . . .

And taking up a breath-still stance
   beneath the wooden bridge,
This soft white,
   snow white,
      feather white statue:
Watcher of the stillness
   and the light.

The Sanctum

A cavern in the green-laced jungle:

While parrots and fruits of sunborne brightness
thrive in the world without,

I live my peace in an inner place
of equal, Eden-like beauty.

From the Cabin Window

Glass bird, you are reflective of the light
  on this wintry March rainy day.
And the violet flowers, the ivory dragons,
  the yellow dried blossoms
    looking down with rounded eye . . . .

A green pasture,
  brown ferns of seasons past . . . .

The trees that rock & swing silently
  beyond the wood of the window-frame . . . .

Bushes of that new spring green,
  a green that never fails to win
  an "Oh!" from winter-weary eyes,
So startled, always,
  by nature's grand renewals . . . .

How can we be jaded to the preciousness,
  when all around it sings?
And we'd beforehand been so blind?

Something to Remember,
Something I Forget

Worrying & working to a frenzy
Make more, not less
About which to worry & work:
Lesson One.

Solution: The Mirror, The Lens

The questions are footprints of wandering thoughts,
And the answers, the paths they make.
Thus we create our own dilemmas --
And our dilemmas their own escape.

Changing

Bending winds, new forgiveness --
The tree grows roots;
The branches feel no pain.

Playing the Waiting Game

Patience:
> it eludes when you're trying,
But when finally acquired
> you forget that it's even there:
For the notion of 'time' --
> a cloud, a ghost --
Seems to silently slip away.

On Truth & Distance

The more perspective,
The more perceptive.

The Ford Yields Philosophy

Sitting in this well-worn pickup,
    metal dusty, pedals worn,
    knobs as functionless as the radio --

Yet it has a personality, impresses me as an entity,
    a creation,
    like the Douglas fir that stands so tall & regal
    beside the window.

Thus man is like a god: he, too, makes Life.

And through our stretch of existence,
    our tenure on this mass of matter
        so filled with possibility,
        rich with varied shapes and resources;

All through our conscious stay on the planet
    we can form, transform, mold new species --
        with paint, words, food, wood,
        music, understanding . . . .

We are constantly putting into the world
    things with form & substance & impact,
Things that can endure -- if only for an instant --
    as a whole that affects the whole
        that surrounds our world.

Our powers are precious;
Our intent must be pure,
So that the products and processes are real --
Real as the magic of the leaf,
                    the wind,
                        the rock;
        the bud,
            the flower,
                the babe.

If our eyes are washed with rain,
        so they clearly see;
If our ears are practiced with listening for
        the subtle, sweet/sad tunes;
If our senses are sharp, and open,
        and mind receptive, supple, alert & mature,
        seasoned and fertile
        and thrusting with ideas --

Then the gift of giving Life
        will bear sweet fruit.

It's Not in Webster's

Peace:

    a place of the heart.

Heart:

    a wand of the hand.

Hand:

    a movement of faith.

Faith:

    a breath of the willing.

The Choice

In the wilderness of freedom,
   in the vastness of our mental landscape,
Mountains thrust;
Valleys freeze;
Oceans brim & bluster.

In the wilderness of freedom, too,
Freshening cheeks in the wind;
Mountains leap;
Valleys clover;
Oceans hum & whisper.

Many a mind has puzzled over
   the why of our two-toned existence;
Many a poet
   penned the paradoxical thought.
And still, the dualities reign supreme:
   changing 'tit' to 'tat'
   and 'up' to its neighbor 'down'.

The trick is to learn
   to turn the coin to your advantage:
Stand on your head,
   and a frown will look like a laugh!

Beneath the Skin

Life is splendor,
    if you mascara, paint & powder --
        no blemishes showing,
        darling . . . .

Life is Celestial Tea and group massage --
    or rollers in your hair,
    a '55 Chevy:
        the diversions,
        the blindfolding games
        are all the same.

But deep in the hollow of my heart,
    I remember the poor, the weak, the dying --
        and those who weep
        bear each letter of my name.

The Tumbling

After walking that tightrope for months,
So well-balanced it seemed like ground
     beneath my feet,
Suddenly --
     I look down, begin to wobble,
       and nearly fall as I thrust out my arms,
         flailing the empty air.

This, dear children,
     is called depression --
Otherwise known as grand funk.

But when the fairy grandmother fails to appear
     and offer her magic wand;
When even one's alter ego abandons ship;
When teeter-totter is more than a game,
     but a matter of desperate survival;
When giddiness gives way
     to a wail of despair --

When . . . .
Then . . . .
What?

Trial by Nature's Fire

Pain:
   white-sheeted and pale,
   ravage-faced, sullen, persistent;

Yet the will to dance again,
   to be whole and safe and real --
   the undiluted insistence --

Propels us, like the wind,
   to ride above the gnashing waves --
      impels us,
      like a river,
      to survive.

The Meaning

Flowers do not shed their scent,
Nor drop their petals,
Before the sun,
      the sky of pearls,
           the breath of soil
Have joined the suite
      with chords, flourishes, harmonies.

Likewise,
      the end of human life comes not
Before someone has seen that soul
      for the golden light
           it truly is.

Coffins close not the experience --

One known,
      once loved,
The living fulfills
      what death seems to take away.

Reflections

I.

Life steps in where it's bidden — and we do the inviting. A nod of the head, instead of the old dour look, accomplishes wonders — life loves a vigorous reception. Who is to blame if tedium rules? Change attitude, change action — and make an adventure of it all. It may be an adventure of the mind, or senses, or dream places. But wherever we choose to allow ourselves to go, however we design our episodes, let them fly.

II.

Life is so extraordinary, that to articulate any one insight, any one condition of being, any one state of social affairs, is to invite immediate contradiction . . . .

As though the process refuses to be crystallized, and rebels at the mind's attempt to do so by veering the opposite way, dancing around the language net cast to catch it, laughing at analysis, theory, even simple designation . . . .

And all the time, 'tis Life that wins out — never our meager formulations of that surpassing, magical unfolding that sweeps all mental forms away.

III.

The wonder of it all is that we can keep from constantly sighing in perplexity or collapsing in despair. What keeps us buoyant when waves are crashing all around us -- bringing news of torment, knowledge of a thousand different forms of contradiction, challenges to our every certitude? The right and wrong, the just and inhumane, the truth and falsehood -- pillars under all the temples have fallen, and the bricks pile up in a vast, confusing heap. Who can sort it out? Who can determine, with a calmness, though the eyes behold phantoms and shadows, chimeras and mistaken identities? Where are the hard choices, the clear paths? Where are the facts without dilemma?

And yet . . . . Above it all, within it all, below and behind it all, we live. We advocate, adhere, advance; question, change course, correct ourselves. We ride the bumps, veer the corners, jump the cliffs -- without cracking. Though thoughts may shatter, preconceptions and speculations flying like shards, we try again. . .forever trying.

And withdrawals from the fray -- for short time periods at the very least -- are not only allowed, but needed. The breather lets us smile once again.

If the World Would End

Tonight, frisbee antics
As the fireflies light the humid, warm fields
Like yellow blinking stars,
Luminous, gleamed.

Sounds of horses clop-clopping on the highway:
The Pennsylvania Dutch go by,
Black garbed, incredibly serious --

While we,
Mimicking discus throwers
Of some novel night-time Olympiad,
Leap high and higher, legs askew,
Arms wild to catch the magic plastic plate . . .
Ducking through space,
Diving, cavorting
With all the impossible gestures
Of young people out on a summer's eve.

Post-game rap 'round the kitchen table:
What would you do if you knew the world
Would end in just three days?

I answer first:
"Kiss everybody!"

It's Not the Straight & Narrow

Yes, it's all so much stranger
   than I conceived
      when I was a child.

Life --
   who can master its mystery,
      fathom its depths?

Mazes, crevices, crannies, nooks --
   there hide the unseen tricks;
Like a pretzeled contortion of logic,
   a chain that defies any try at following
      from 'a' to 'b' --

My God, what a train of unscheduled events!
What a cockeyed tune to dance to!

Taking Aim

Can I live without a dash of red,
   a dab of blue,
     a gash of gold,
The brush of passion splashed across my canvas?

Can I live without the dazzle-dance,
   the starry swirl,
     the sunrise pearl
To cut the veil of darkness?

Otherwise, I'm pallid, pale,
   unsung, unflung, unseeing:
A gray-eyed thing,
   unborn, unfelt, unreal.

Assert the right,
Acclaim the height,
Exclaim the legacy: Light!
Unchained, unnamed, uncaged,
A searing flame fire-tongued
And roaring.

And so I do not linger
Like cold wash out on a line,
Or dangle like a dried old leaf
Wattling in the wind --

But add intention to the fire's fuel,
   desire and deepened yearning,
Urge on the flames,
   encourage the leaps
   of liquid, hot-lipped gold.

Where green is fading far away,
   tread not, go way beyond;

Where sapphire blue has turned to ash,
   fling off, push back, strike down;

Where flowers wilt, where breeze is stilled,
   where creek is strangled dry --

This place is Lie: I seek to live The True.

Toward the Free

We are limited
    only by
    the contents of our conceptions,
    the contents of our perceptions --

And liberated by both.

Passage

As the nightfire deepens,
    and the clay becomes
        a fine-grained golden dust;

As the laughter sings softly,
    in a hue unknown in youth --
        but no less wondrous;

As the mystery is solved,
    yet the mist enshrouds
        and shadows once again;

As the red-winged bird
    shatters mind-made plans
        but delivers our heart-warm dreams;

As we live and breathe,
    Time becomes the teacher:
        and our eyes,
        with lines of age,
        begin to See.

New-Found Land

Coming into consciousness --
    a life steeped in the tea leaves
    of an extraordinary warm sweetness,
A drink so palatable and mesmerizing
    that the liquid soars around the cave of the brain,
    like a softly petaled potion,
    rocking, luxurious.

And onto the threshold it brings us,
    fingers clasping with wings of wind;
Into the current, out past the islands
    of myth and fear and pain . . . .

And with exultant release we sail past the plans
    of a brow-knitted, cold December --

Sail away on the waves
    of a rosy-blushed sea:
Sun rising, spring-leaved, on the shore.

New Muse

How do we live our lives?
Out of habit,
Or like rabbits
Out of a hat?

Magicians' tricks
Are much more fun
Than anchors --

Pull 'em up,
Move 'em out --
And play!

A Newer Testament, Old As the Hills

The <u>real</u> scripture is --

Just one big paragraph, saying
   "Love Everyone."

Cliffchance

To the precipice!
The jutting point past which the world's
    unhung,
        unrung,
            air-free,

And breath & thought have to wing it,
    to fly --
        or fall.

Fantasia

Captured in the Zanzibars of time,
Emulating sapphires
Of the succulent vine,
A sheik of the ruby jungle trail.

Captured in the Xanadu of love,
Seeing lions leaping after cubs
And leopards sleeping,
Birds of ancient plumage,
Golden speaking.

Allegories of purple,
Yellow-orange amber,
Orchestrated birds & sun,
Razzamatazz and fire.

Pheasants bow to peacocks,
Feathers stride and nod,
Floral wreathes embrace the trees
With drops of petaled blood.

Moonlight's scythe of saber white
Slicing hearts and stars,
Rising 'cross a scarlet sea --
Parting the waters of glory.

*

But any such shaded,
Non-bumpy path
Is bound someday
To hit the groves
Of uneven brush,
The stones of hills & folly.

Asunder, above
The timberline,
Hurricane hawks,
Beak-sharp, stark,
Deserted,
Desert-drawn --

Well I know,
And well I forget,
It always goes thus
And Thus.

Man:Woman -- treat delight;
But of all the adjacent beggars,
There's always the tears on verge,
On edge --
The ledge over which to fall.

*

Yet here on the slopes of "illusion"!
Mirage of willows,
Thirsty-drench glens,
The banner obeys life's call.
Abracadabra --
Ferns are lacy,
I'm facing only
A kiss.

And what surprises
Await us!
Giving way to specials,
Buying them 'cause
They encounter you shopping --
Keep you hopping
From store to store,
From sky blue, breathe,
To ecstacy furred,
Magnificent.

*

For who can depart
From the undulating mysteries,
The tiny berries
And sweeps of storm?

Renounce the victory
Of wings over water?
Never!
If God pretends,
Let me linger in the fancy:
The dream was never sweeter.

So sing, unclouded, uncorked & screwy,
Unmake the beds
As the rolling begins,
And layers of arousal
Balloon and collapse,
Ocean eddies.

Heroics of passion,
Ember-chambered love,
Diminishing fog
In the burning sun --

We leave a clear-washed mirror:
Glasswax couldn't do better.

Reach the Emerald Isle,
Reach Manhattan Island --
O current of the strong-denoted bliss!
Blitz the trails
With leaves of bronze,
The echo-blue of morning
By the shore.

*

Eat well.

Eat well.

Eat tree and brook

And sound of the sand, of sea

In the afternoon sun.

Reconstitute

This juice of being,

Thrown into a package of people

We call "the world" --

Or is it "whirled"?

"Leapin' Lizards!"

Said Orphan Annie,

Orange curls, hollow eyes

In perpetual surprise.

Convoys of wares,

Of dream-wares

Coat my M & M's with fun,

And I defer the pompous brow

To another one.

*

'Tis a current tale,

One which all but melts the edges

Of ice cream cones,

And otherwise stimulates
Appetite's tongue.

And how often,
I wonder,
Will the animate world
Twirl on its hurling course,
To be roasted by sun
In a shish-kebab life --
Ah, but the sauce
Is yours.

*

Oh, captured in the Zanzibars of time,
Emulating sapphires
Of the succulent vine,
A sheik of the ruby jungle trail.

Captured in the Xanadu of love,
Seeing lions leaping after cubs
And leopards sleeping,
Birds of ancient plumage --
Golden seeking!

In One

I looked down upon my self,
    in the arms of someone who has given me
    his precious treasure --

And my heart's barriers,
Walls of ice I didn't even know were there,
    came down;
Thawed by the presence of a warmth so full,
    so out of the ordinary,
That all I could do was feel,
    silence enraptured;
Feel and let him feel,
    hand on my shoulder, skin-touching,
      the same as mine on his --
Whose body, no matter;
Whose soul, the same.

This singleness, the miracle,
    a special gift of love:
      dissolver of all bounds,
      creator of all bonds.

A Touch of the Glory

In lakes,
     in reflected forests green,
         deep green,
         life-green;
In eyes that are pure,
     angelic,
         vulnerable --
We visit the Special Realm.

The feel in our fingers,
     tingled;
         omened,
         the bounce in our toes --
Dancing, winking at paradise
     with a wave of the hand,
         a way of the deep blue night.

Laugh, and let your belly expand,
     sing, stretch out your throat,
And fling your arms,
     unspiraling
         to the sunset skies
         and aqua-shimmer seas.
For it comes and it goes,
     we glimpse and forget --

Evanescence is a pleasure:
     watch the flame.

Of Those Less-Than-Idyllic Habits
Of Your Enamored: Two Views

1.

You've got to have fortitude to be a lover:

To endure,

Through and past,

The annoyances assuming enormous proportions,

The quirks that irk,

The follies that stick out their tongues

Right under your nose --

Yes, you've got to have lots of iron

To beef up that sweet lover's heart of gold!

2.

You forget when you forgive;

And when in love,

You can't help it!

The Legacy

The pain and the joy --
    so close, so crazily close,
Like twins of Will and Won't
    dancing duets
        inside my breast --

The sensual fragrance lingers,
    the velvet glove & flame arousing skin,
        caressful places;

But so does the loss, the lack of love
    live on.

While poets toss out image-pearls
    in lyrical justification,
And philosophers play with an abacus
    of verbal beads and clues --

Neither can erase or ease
    the paradox
        of the heart.

The Hard Part

Edges creep up slowly,
Like shadows on a lawn --
And we devour our despair
By slowly reaching for the sleek, lean moon,
Ascending in an arc above our heads.

Never before have I wept and sung
With one full tongue,
Polishing the rough-chiseled thrusts
Of my blade --

For solace is found in moves of the heart,
Expansions of lung,
Vigor of muscle.

And it is not mournful to bury
A flower's fallen petals
In the rich, dark loam and humus.

For who can surmise
The temper of the future?
Don't close the books
On this time in life,
This continuing song
Drawn out like a long trombone --

Though all you've got is a lonely smile,
And rainbow tears, and faith --

And a silver-gemmed desire
Cut to bone.

Do I Try Again At Another Love?

To live by experience --
    taking one's lessons seriously,
    as reflections thrown up
    by the mirror of the past
    so we can truly see our selves;
Yet not to become entrapped
    within the web of our conclusions,
Or shrink for fear of "getting hurt again,"
Or leap to impulsive dreams.

Sometimes it seems so obvious --
    how to Be.
Sometimes we're finely honed
    like the needle of a phonograph:
    "in the groove,"
    playing music to perfection.
But when confusion, not clarity,
    makes choices hard to follow;
When uncertainty blows its chilly, northern winds;
When trying hard doesn't seem to work,
    nor letting things "just happen";
When all the rivers lead to the sea,
    but their source, the mountain springs,
    still strongly beckon --

The heart must wait,
    and patience take the lead.

Facts of the matter

1.

Can I cry?
For what?
For self-deception, illusion, delusion,
The mask I wrought, sought & wore?
The mask of a child's "always and forever" --
Torn off by an adult's parting sigh.

2.

I am
My own fool,
And an old fool at that.

3.

The pain of rejection,
The pain of reflection --
Yet still the sun winks in my eye.

Rendezvous

I wanted him to meet me
With a gesture of passion,
As tho on the eve of some great burst of spring
About to color the meadow
With thousands of glorious petals.

I wanted him to say all those things
That the deepest whispers of one's heart sing
In the lonely night and the hollow of the day.

It had been my dream for years,
My cherished anticipation --
For who can surrender a hope as vast as the sea?

But my eyes could not deceive me,
Nor could his lips.
When I finally clasped those hands I missed,
Put my eager face to his cool, calm cheek --
The answer to my quest was all too clear.

Funny, how disappointment can free the heart!
I sang good-bye to the past in an instant,
Bade my good old dreams farewell;
And glided, sans remorse or tears,
Toward the opening door --
The opening heart to come.

A Simple Prescription

Give --
And forgive.
Love --
And be loved.
The motions of our hearts
Are there to be sought,
Sifted like sand
Through our tears.

The Continuance

Emerging from the crucible
Of love's disappointment --
A scalding cauldron of emotion,
A burning brew of despair is <u>not</u> the outcome.
Instead, a freshness and new aliveness,
As after passage under a thundering waterfall,
Skin & eyes & hair exposed to the pounding drops
That once were sweet dew
And ascended skyward,
Descending as rain coalesced
In an edge-leaping stream.
For my body is a mountain,
And high I have climbed, and <u>been</u> climbed.
Yet the peaks still beckon,
My head turns cloudward --
Lungs exalting air of stellar space
And star-paced motion.
Conceptions of "higher awareness"
Can scarcely come close to the senses I feel --
The magic of daily existence defies
The most far-fetched notions of dreams.
And here, as though the fires of life
Were ablaze with logs of mammoth, endless fuel,
Here inside my eyes that see more
Than my mind has words to express,
In the midst of this whirlpool, this maelstrom,
This hurling hurricane-eye of being --
I sing like the sea.

Wing

The bird that leapt like a blue-green featherflame
thru my heart took off; reached the sky, danced a
bit, then descended in a long, sweeping arc that
scooped through the grove of orange trees, and
ended right in the middle of the buttercups in front
of the yard. I breathed with a soft eagerness,
tasting the spring of the day: it was sweet with that
greenness of purpose that makes all growing a thing
of great gasping in suprise.

At last! I could look forward to his arms' clasp
each night, his dearness of skin, his touch that made
the searching, the quest and hope, no longer needful.
I was loved, and I loved — with a smile for the luck
and for the past, a moistness of tear.

Eve of Another Lifetime

Long after we arrived,
The darkness followed;
But who cared whether dawn we sipped
Or dusk . . . .
As we lingered,
Long as the heart allowed,
In silky, longtime passion.

In the pool of fevered love,
Deep as a well,
We dipped with the pull and flow
Of pulsating breath
That carried us up the valley.

Like a starling,
Mountainous summer
Dove through canyons and curving cliffs
And all the bends of the rolling river.

Melodious hills,
Kneeling in surrender --
Thickly a blanket of time.

And tho life may not be
Cream & sugar --
Look for the honey,
The clear-warm, amber flow.

The Ideal

Give me hope:
That the last will be best,
And the best,
Last.

Another "He" I Try

Perhaps we can tip-toe balance
'Twixt the trust of being one,
And the romance of being two.

90.

Voyage

Take me to the shore:
I want to sit there and smell the sea,
    the sand,
        see the waterbirds dive & winging . . . .

Taste the salty tang,
    hear the roar of the foam,
        and the ocean's insistent command --

To cast my soul,
    once more,
        off shore,
To set my soul
    a-sailing.

And again the ship of fools,
And again the fool's desire,
And again I board,
    a willing-mate
        of love.

Hawaiian I

The luscious me of pineapples,
    honeybrown sand,
Cherryskin lips
    sipping milky dawn's vapor,
Junglebirds winkling
    a silverstar green:
Their songs are my eye's
    jeweled bells.

Desire

Your flesh
Speaks
Like tiptoe colors
Of dusky evening sky,
And silky yellow clouds
And tapfire moon . . . .

Sighing reeds,
The clues
Of sailing night.

Signature

You are a lake,
    and I pour onto your wavetop
        like a trickling of stars --

Just to light up the foam,
    gleam it a bit,
        dust it with gems & pearls
          from the heavens,

And then with a luminous pen,
    I sign
        the silver-lined name of
        Love.

The "Ah!" Again

We met;
    whispered in filmy, dawn-like words,
    our colors blending softly, hushed
    as we tilted our lips toward each other's eyes,
    and our hearts toward the open sky.

Light drew its gauzy veil around us
    as we ceased interpreting,
    cleaving to conceptions,
And hung suspended in that eye of stillness,
    that eye of silence
    known to candle's flame,
    petals in wind,
    waves cool and blue-green,
    lovers.

We become no one but the Presence surpassing,
    like a droplet of water,
    a droplet of light --
    motion encapsuled
    in a skin
    of motionless time.

And as water does not blare out words
    but silently shares in light's repose,
In quietude
    we let the moment speak.

All Metaphors Do Not Equal

My heart, my home, my man:
Loving you is bottomless,
   succulent,
      tremendous --
I lounge, lavished
   in rose-stroked hues.

Guitar strings ring
   with my song to your ears,
That hear me, hear my
   voice of soul.

Deeper we fly
   till cosmos-wide,
Hurling eagle-winged sails
   to peaks
      spiraled in sky-flowers.

My essence revolves
   'round your essence revolving
      'round lips of your eyes,
         my love.

Threading through me
   you lilt and weave
      a heart-flow, love-flow,
         shower of life.

How thicketed the foliage
  of my feeling-forest for you,
How green/yellow tinted
  the palette of my love stream!
Drink of me darling,
  your spring of softness shall I be
    for eons of love,
    for eons of love.

Like yellow sunshine you warm me,
Like clear, cool rain
  you rinse thru my flesh,
Like whole notes of aqua
  you play a space/time jam.

And how can a calf express its joy
  at drinking mother's milk?
Or a cloud sing out its sky-love?

Brocades, velvets, satins, pearls --
  your love clothes me
  with more radiance & splendor.

Rippled masses of seashells
  on the beaches of my soul,
    you are,
    my love.

Loveshot

A catapult of dreams,
An arrow shot --
Your bow of love --
Has hit its mark
Inside my heart,
On target,
Right on fire.

The Apex

We are vaulted to the ends of the universe --
   and our passions are not amiss,
   our wheels not bound by road maps,
   our entering zest mixed with nectar & wine.

And we go to the sexual jungle
   to eat of the fruits of the sleek maroon,
   the bites of orange,
   grabs of red,
   the silver-splash wave
   on a white-flaming shore.

Encased, enrolled in levels of pleasure,
   of fortune, and touch, and yearning --
Pursuing desires with eyes fully conscious,
   lips in a mutual melting --

Unpretentious,
   rambunctious,
     voluptuous,
       tempestuous,
Fire-limbed, swelled to the brim --

We open and reach for the ecstacy potion,
   the motion so wild --
     so free.

Still a Mystery to Myself

Once again tossed --
    flung from jaw-bite steel
To willows,
    scent,
       enhancement --

These moods and swings,
Sways of a willful blood
    and a playful heart!

Yes, it's hard to keep one's perspective:
To conceive when you're up
    why you've ever been down,
And when down,
    to believe in the up!

High Fashion

Lace-wearing, I opted for jeans;
Jeans-jaded, I went to silks, brocades.
Then nudity took its hold --
The dare of bare skin.

For how could I clothe my soul?
Wear garments with truth, not pride?

And so I returned to Self alone --
To the place with no place to hide.

A Simple Equation

She who gives all
    gets that back --
And more!

The Gift

I spoke to the mountains:
Told the leaves of my presence,
Skies of my purpose,
Stones of my worries.
I breathed the golden air of the sun,
And lent my heart to the butterflies;
Dined on visions of green-leaved things,
And scents of woodland flowers.

And in return, I learned;
Gained in respect;
Felt more than books could ever impart.
I became solid, and songful,
Retuned, retrained
In hearing my own true Self.
I began thinking anew,
Fresh as snow,
Moon-bright & rightly paced.

I was blessed,
And counting,
I thanked.

In Truth

Can the flame, begotten

    of inner lights

    in inner caves,

    inner sights

    and inner stars,

    mind & heart

    in rhythmed reunion --

Can the flame, begotten

    ever be forgotten?

Gotten rid of

    by "explanations," "refutations,"

    scientists attempting to

    Skinner it away?

"It's all in the mind," they say --

    or the soul, Jung replies.

For what is more dear:

    near the heartbeat of life,

    near the whole,

    the hearth,

    the Goal?

Having Leaped

We are the way of the Crown:
    kingly.
And the Shepherd:
    with green.
And the Queen,
    feminine, soft,
        shapely as a hill-flank.

The jewels hang from our ears --
    wearing pearls on bare lobes,
    softly formed
    as they catch the moon shining.

Lifting our heads -- limitlessly . . . .
Walking atop the spire (we aspire),
Mosques golden-tipped,
    golden-domed,
    golden peaking --

Waltzing in time.
    with Time.

Rasmussen Bay

To the madrone
    with its carpet of moss yellow-green,
To the leaf-strewn grass,
    and bark of dark brown,
To the gray twigs rested,
    and resting,
    serene,
To the blue-tipped bushes,
    sea-blown.

And here the cliff
    is both wild and friendly,
Sun a late guest,
    barely known,
Fog rushing in,
    licking-smooth-silent,
And gull wings the ocean,
    towards home.

December Eve

A quiet night,
Snow covers us all around --

Green arms swaying under heavy white cloaks,
Grasses blanketed, branches of lace,
Pathways gone beneath powdery white:
Crunchable under foot, feathery in hand.

A hawk, wide-winged, uplifts with power,
High above white's hush . . . .
Small dark sparrows, cheeping,
In the search for bits of food . . . .
Heron, black sleek grace upon a red buoy,
Harbor bobbing,
Contented 'mid the gray-white roll of seas.

Islands shining white,
Sandcliffs, hills,
Brushed with frosty dreams . . . .
Tangerine tinge to the sunset west,
And above, a cobalt blue --

Living in the woods
Of winter's finest, freshest moments.

Coast

The sand sparkles like fairy dust from a generous magical wand -- sunlight turning each grain into a golden, glassy gem, moonlight changing the gems to silver. By the ocean, wide-sweeping and blue-green frothy, the logs sit placidly -- they have come to rest at the shore. Enter the sky-soaring creatures: seagulls, hawks and eagles, each watching the sea while swimming the air. Bobbing up and down, the black sleek heads of seals; to the east, a boat with snow-white sails and crimson hull. The wind scoops and tumbles and oscillates, a whimsied prancing; the fish feel only the liquid currents below, the depths -- invisible to our eye.

And nature encompasses the whole, and we call it Coast: gelatinous colors, films and mists, crags and splashing surfs. It all belongs, and we to it -- the sea at the fringe of the land.

The Lifting

Have you heard the green color of purpose,
   the horn of command sing its trumpet
      in the morning dewcolors?
And taken the boat upon its blue-brown seascape
   for a turn at wind's jostle, push,
      glint-the-sun games?

There, there the mountain rises:
   green and steep,
      oblivious of rocks' sharpness.
For upthrust, resonance,
   sky-seeking grace and grandeur
      call courage from its rest upon the lambskin rug,
         boudoired and bored --

Into Action:
   passion pouring cymbals of sound,
      glimpses of memory, inks of nightsparkle --
      pen-dipped gilt and gleam.

O, sky! O dark star-bed, deep as your eyes!
Begin to light the lamp of the heart!
Call me to your fire!
The jewels of glossy altitude,
   come with your satin stroke,
      your sweet caress!

Again, The Quest/The Question

What of the quest for holiness?
The wandering within, to touch --
One's self,
One's soul,
One's deepest consciousness --

All in touch with the worlds & lives
And living molecules
Beyond us,
Within us . . . .

The effort, the attention,
The exceptional rewards --

Yet how far are we from our goal?

Always receding, of necessity:
As our aims are lifted higher,
Sky-fearlessly high,
By wings of ideals --

As we see,
With ever more clarity,
What could constitute such a thing
As "god-hood" --
Or at least human happiness.

And so, as in Zeno's Paradox,
We run and run and run,
Never crossing the finish line --

Ah yes, but look back
To the hills of the past,
To the treks, the marches,
The giving.
Not bad, thus far,
Between ache and grief,
Not bad: much more
Of Living.

And I write the agenda
For my future of days:
To rise from the kneel,
And to kneel back, thanking;
To loft, to launch,
To land on the ground --
Not merely guessing
At what is Divine.

Light/Delight

Mountain greens --
    velvet blanket for naked feet,
    the sweet & secret blades of intoxication.
The foliage is a canopy;
Stars upon my head
    a winking tiara.

And only when we open up
    to the fullest permeation --
Suffusion of skin as pores absorb,
    drink in & relish the balm --

Can we know the nuanced entunement,
    feel the preciousness, the allurement,
Wrap in a fragrance that never regrets,
    forgets,
        or fails.

The ring is worn like an emblem,
    a visible sign of the start of the journey --
Traversing without geography, time limits,
    compass or provisions --
A free-wheeling, free-feeling lifting.

And the truth is contained as in a kernal:
The essence, the sap in a pearl
    about to ease & trickle,
    like a thin, pink cloud at sunset,
        toward our eyes.

Going Through

Each one of us has her pains & processes, means of moving thru the alternating joys and weaknesses of being human. The jungle is thick with marshes and magnificent sunsets, foliage and moments of green ecstacy; but the deserts alike have their moods.

We endure them all. The key is the quality — the "how" in which we travel, the shape of our caravan: downcast, bitter, upset and vengeful (destructive of self or others, it's all the same); or wide-eyed, open, knowing with conscious fervor and crisp, supple clarity. We cannot throw away the facts — they persist, whether smiling or not. And we cannot pursue delusions (though a hope on wing is absolutely essential).

Better to take the bitter pill with the sweet — to feel the actual pain, not wash the heart with fakery.

Yet we must keep believing that indeed, our freedom can follow not far behind.

There Burns an Inner Flame

It will not do to pretend,
To close my eyes,
   play hide and go seek,
To dull out, numb out,
   anesthetize the mind,
For a purpose that my brain decides,
   arbitrarily,
   is "real."

The other hand should take the wheel,
   follow the inner cues:
Events of the present dovetailing
   heart's true path.

This means change, this means choosing,
   this means affection for my Self.
What more can one ask of life,
   than the freedom to grow?
To breathe the air of exaltation --
   not stuffy rooms we cage ourselves into,
   lock ourselves into with chained attachments . . . .

All for some "reason," some "logic"
   pulled from a book
   or someone else's hat.

We're given eyes, ears, hands and feet,
And organs of self-direction.
But to also allow that "third force" to appear,
Not connected with use of muscle or bone,
Or the autonomous system
    that runs our machine of flesh --

To give that arrow the tension to launch,
To splash the sun and spark the target,
To feel the flux-run of oceans,
    sea bodies tracking our soul's true seasons . . . .

To actually be what the saints and philosophers
    and children all believe --

This is the moment of waking truth,
    the instant of blessing's perspective.

And I don these spectacles, and I praise them.
And I put on my cloak of luminosity,
Take off my fears of tin,
Soak my wounds in liquid,
    dipping,
And dab laugh's rouge on my cheeks . . . .

How the aura leaps and caresses!
How the bird of value sings!
How the ebony/gold
Brings life a higher contrast!

All in the name of passion,
All in the name of calm,
All in the name of tears that fall,
Joys that smile,
Singers and lovers,
Dancers and winds and calls --

I hear the sound of a voice
That has no name.

Struck

Lavender appears,
    suddenly,
        crystallized --

As tho darkest night
    tumble-bursting with thunderclap clouds
        had never existed, persisted,
        gritted my teeth
        with months of reeling torture.

Golden veils of sheerest light
    now scamper 'round my veins,
Flowers jeweled, garlands, chimes --

And all the thoughts of winter
    pass away.

Daydream

Lying among Greek columns
    in spring-bud relaxation,

I crochet Mozart with
    piano keys
    of white twine and pink silk thread.

Night Crossing

Journey over a moonless sea,
    past moonless peaks,
    dark-washed horizon;
Boat a satellite gliding thru space,
    the place of void beyond motion.

Nothing exists but the deep-breathing breeze,
    the muscles that pull and ease,
The paddles dipping,
    stirring,
    scattering gems of droplets
    like splash-lumined stars.

But isn't this really the icy deep,
    with power of death
    at the depth of its fingers?
My mind can conceive
    what my heart can't believe --
That beneath this silky-black spell
    there leaps a danger
    at bone-chilling fathoms.

Yet Beauty, not Beast,
    is all I can see --
And willingly would I die, fulfilled
    by the peace I feel in the jewel-calm sea
    of her splendor.

Lund

An early-ending day in November
    is a time of cold, gray rains,
    enclosed silence,
    and stretching imagination.

Wide glass window of a dimming, blue-lit sky
    reveals leaves, tree trunks, ferns.
Stove roars its heat; lamplight dances;
    candle awakens to its dawn.
A chocolate-brown cup and a round white bowl
    sit quietly, side by side;
Letters are finished, feet wool-shod;
The wood is chopped and piled --
And no visitors knock at this forest cabin door.

But aloneness tonight is not really lonely:
A wand is waved,
And Love comes, softly treading,
To enter the hearth of my home.

Oregon Woods

Down in the hollows,
Beneath the towering trees --
A glimpse of a life
Belled and wished and seeded by a dream.
The hand touches moss,
And smoothly strokes the petals . . . .
Birds gather softly,
To peek and peck
And wander thru needles of cedar
Carpeting the soil.

The grass breathes the moistness
Of early morning dew . . . .
And the river-water whistles,
Seaming & spurring thru nooks
In the serpentine stones.
Clouds in a muted shadow-show,
Sunlight falling dappled and longingly,
Tempting the leaves to experience more
When the time rounds into noon.

In the bed of the brook, varicolored pebbles
Gleam with constant cleansing.
The eastern alders lean,
Ever listening toward the sun.
And kissing with the lips of fullest splendor,
Cherry-red and cherry-sweet,
The fragrance of vine-wild berries
On the cheek of Madame Day.

The Gem

Waking up to the sound of the roosters crowing, the sight of graceful cedar boughs outside my window -- greenness surrounds, and life blooms. One miracle turns into another; the circle revolves and sings a song of entunement, a song of clarity, beauty, and special awareness that makes living a magical unfolding . . . an exceptional, intimate sharing . . . a pure, precious way of giving and receiving. The diamond sparkles.

Learning and relearning the name of the game: truth resides in opening the heart to all, in acting and feeling as One -- yet at the same moment being your individual evolved Self. No fears, no barriers to the world . . . God speaks through many lips, and greets with many eyes. Seeing on the faces of men, women, children, babes, that luminous, clear expression, as a forest pool reflects the pines, the sun, the sky . . . . Thriving on the scents, harmonies, hues of a reality beyond the mundane, beyond the rushed and worried commonplace passage of everyday time . . . . Immersion in a sea of holy being, a heaven on earth as crystalline pure, white-shining as the stars.

How can we always attain this sense of being fully, sparklingly alive? By staying sensitive to the cues offered by the structure of events; by keeping in touch with the guideposts of subtle feeling that mold one's responses gently, as the wind sculpts the cliffs of sand . . . . A calm knowing, and unpretentious humility. Sweetness is a spring that always flows.

It is not all play -- work is very much the fiber that holds the weave of this tapestry together. But work done with exuberance, with respect for necessity and a love of moving muscles, circulating blood as red as the rising sun; work done in the spirit of wanting to be part of the natural spin of energy, the same energy that revolves the planet and does not stop or hesitate in order to question why, to balk or complain. Yet it is not a machine-like mode of action -- humanity and grace are stamped in its very core. One wants to do what is "right," for what is right is what is fitting -- as fitting that a rose should smell like a rose, the ocean lap the shore with constant music.

And the thoughts inside one's head are not harsh and interruptive, querulous and loud; they blend with the texture, serenely. What is Life, if not such a vision to see? Why be born, eat, sleep, and die, if not to find and touch and really know? Moonstreams light up the waters by night; sun-gold shapes the day. And we can sip, taste the celestial dew as luscious as mother's milk, and the primal kiss . . . . We can feel the pink dawning clouds on our cheeks, stroll with the luted warblings of birds, dance like the newest leaves caressing the earth and sky . . . . All in All.

These words, written after five days of encampment at another gathering -- a gathering of those who try to Be, as truly as they can; those who hold as the treasure of their hearts the treblings of the brook, the arc of blue, the wine of unselfish devotion. Each time a petal lifts from the clustered bud, opens its eyes to the waiting light; each time a hand feels the essence of another; each evening that strokes the ending day, covers it softly with the jeweled cape of black and velvet night; each filament, strand, thread of the silken gown worn by silver-dropped fields of grass, deliciously wet on bare toes and winding 'round the mind like a sphere in the heavens; each season, each reason, each note in the melody; each look of trust -- a tinkle of glass chimes, a swash of color from the sacred brush, another affirmation of the divine.

The Touch

The sunlit, melting snow-jewels
    tickled my palm --

  Spring at hand.

The Purpose.

Lanterns in the mind,
    flames inside the heart;
Everywhere the means of luminescence.
Sparks, glowing, roundness, expansion --
The rolling of the sun.

We orbit our imagination like a crystal satellite --
    to pick up waves, celestial ripples,
    heart-dances of the stars . . . .
Then carry back the legacy,
    a silken purse
    with coins of truest worth.

Dante retrieved; so did the saints.
Stepping forward, golden-slippered . . . .
    and returning to grass and children --
    by the sway of the shoulder,
    the smile, the eyes,
        to convey.
For the voyage embarks constantly,
    and the ocean seethes with experience;
        the rainbows gather, a color congregation:
Put your arms about them --
    the angels are your friends!

All's Well That Augurs Well

Amorous possibilities
Pour strawberries down my mind,
Sneak lemondrops in my wine,
Play Mozart suites in samba time.

Amorous possibilities
Draw aces on my bones,
Etch faces on ice cream cones,
Light stony nights with sun-glow poems.

The Master

Monet: strokes with a magic brush,
        layering colors that pray, blend,
        melt, excite,
        dance with vibrant elation
           or calmest repose.

Monet: vision of light,
        palette of eye,
        secret of style.

Monet: renders for humans
        angelic gardens,
        blue-green mists, streams,
        suns of an other-worldly range . . . .

With nothing less
        than fully-astonished rapture
        as his goal.

A Meditation

Giving
    Loving
        Creating
            Appreciating,

Synthesizing
    Observing
        Open
            Without guile,

Balancing
    Believing
        Sensing
            Receiving,

Hoping
    Trusting
        Letting go
            Your smile.

Celebrity / Celebration

True fame
Is being as happy to meet yourself
As Brando, Streep or Redford --
Or a bird, a sunrise, a mountain.

Pretty Little Maid

O, flower in the weeds --
Why does your presence surprise me,
Delight me,
More than a hundred of your companions,
Growing prettily in a row?

The Party

I walked into the blue room, silk-enclosed skin connecting with smooth walls, flowers on mahogany polished tables, pointed lights of glass-spangled chandeliers. I was as consonant with my surroundings as a flutist and a bird; therefore I was calm and clear-cheeked and high-spirited.

By the broad window, a statue of a long, lithe woman — marble, white, graced — marked the spot. I strode with a gentle river-motion, and stood at enough of a distance from her so that neither she nor I detracted from the other's beauty. We watched the heads nod, the shoulders swing, the eye-laughs come and go. It was an interaction in which no brutality could survive; no insensitivity be bred. People listened and felt; they believed.

Gradually the music came to a mid-evening interval, and the words became more audible. The commonality, intelligence, and sincerity of the guests could only make my heart glad — no feeling of loneliness at watching, unengaged in the goings-on. For I was one with the freedom, and the friendliness, the bright glimpses; I was part and parcel of those who experienced and expressed Humanity.

Evening colors lilted through the air, pale golds and soft, pearly tones. The time was ripe for speaking. He looked straight into my self, and I said something smiling and meaningful. We began where the waters meet the sky, unbarred. It was easy to go from there into revelation of our private lives, philosophized exchange, merriment over silly puns, and touching. We were filling up at each other's fountain — and splashed among the frothy droplets with childlike happiness and mature appreciation.

How long the people had been leaving, neither of us could tell; but at some point our eyes focused on the half-vacant room, the dim lights, the quietude. We held each other's arms, and like a wave of sound joining its own harmonic, swept together out the door.

That Place

The meeting of the mouths,
The tasty greeting of the lives of heart,
The healing of the clouds,
The rustled beating of the eyes behind the mind,
Like living embers.

Anew

Almond light,
Mystically motioned
In the lap of a twinkling eve . . . .

Mountains hearing,
Cloaked in starry mantles . . . .

Leaf-strewn breathing,
Lake embrace,
Embroidered sylvan dew . . . .

And then the southward skies unsealing,
Dawn-pasteled,
Cloud-scented . . . .

A petaled pendant
Graced around my neck --

      Like you,
      My love.

Emergence

What began as a thought,
As the stillest, smallest line --
Emerged like a bubble,
Filling my head,
Infusing my being with color . . . .

And I shook my hair,
And breathed clearly
   once again.

What is this perception
That enters my life
   with a whisper, a wave, a gong?
Another cocoon to crack and slough off,
   old feathers to thankfully shed?

Loop-de-loop, I skip the rope
   and jump the looming hurdles,
Flick the switch and hold my breath,
New-tuning to my fate.

Appraising life, I place myself
On the chart of a brand new course:
Trajectory that of the shooting stars --
   coordinates: points of wonder.

Let There Be Life

The calmer, clearer earth-lakes reflect,
Liquidly holding our visions . . . .

Our eyes perceive,
Our minds receive
The snow peaks' flame in the waters --

The flame that gives the knowledge of sight,
The flame that spires the sky,
The flame that is our hymn and wind,
The cause of the leaf's
Green giving --

The urge for our muscles and hearts
To create,
To feel the heat
Of the light,
Flame-white,
Of the Living.

The Spark

The chain unlinks with the snap of liberty,
Anxiety cries out no more --
For the arms of deliciousness open wide,
And in their hearth, like a touchstone,
Lies the burning coal of love.

Not yet quelched by rains of estrangement,
Not yet doused by tears --
It burns, a flame so easy to revive:
One breath and the fire leaps-to.

And that breath was a word,
Logos of creation,
A "Come!" that pierced me
Clear through . . . .
Like the bell-clear strum of a golden guitar,
Like the rub of a velvet bloom
On a velvet face.

And I take out my paintbox,
Uncap the dreams,
Brush riches of purples on walls,
Thank oceans, praise trees,
Fill the fields with affection --
For the space to orbit,
Galaxial,
Gravity-free.

Participant / Observer

How to merge,
  immerse
    in the flowing wave

As drops
  that dance
    with the water;

And emerge,
  still dry,
    when the lifeboat heaves

And heads
  into stormy
    weather --

How to live
  as both a human
    and a god.

Mystery

Bathing
   in unknown psychic waters --
Braving the depths,
   the shadow-plays
      of forces beyond Control . . . .

Floating in seas of silver
   leaning circles upon the gold:

      eyes of young,
      eyes of old,
      eyes of seeing
      what we never can be told.

Metaphor

What is a leaf but a pattern,
Tangible and transient?

And a life?

How to See

Perception:
        hidden 'twixt the yellows
         of the sunshine.

Forest Family

Pinecones --
The babes of those mammoth tree-mothers,
Whose branches,
Unafraid,
Embrace the blue --

And the snowy white stars,
The fogs and the rains,
The scorching sun's heat,
And breathless, still mornings . . . .

Those venerable, deep-rooted women of woods,
Of mountains and moisture
And earth's full, deep soil,
Whose spires, strong-hearted,
Invincibly green,
Inherit the years --

While we humans
Pass away.

A Snail's Pace

Inches,
Tiny parts and subdivided
Inches,
Nature's minute particulars and
Inches,

Drawing small steps closer
To the Measure
And the Measurer.

No Longer Alone

The heart's wait
Will have an answer.

Tho its call is long,
Echoing thru the cool, blue air of night,
Tho rivers, heedless,
Play their silver tunes,
Tho seasons come,
And seasons go,
And snow falls on the branches,
Tho babies cry,
And old men die,
And seekers wander, sightless --

The heart will rise
When called by the secret moon.

Balance

There is no indulgence
That is not counterbalanced --
A shift to the other side.

For to overdo is to have to do over --
To sift through the black after white.

And though Aristotle's Golden Mean
Is scorned as old-fashioned, unsound --

Nature herself teaches
We must seek the middle ground.

How It Goes

Life has its phases of learning,
  repudiating,
    reincorporating,
Then seeing things anew --
The germ of wholeness,
The germ, the seed,
The pearl of a seeking heart.

Undoctrinaire, undogmatic --
  do not confuse taste with the right to judge.
Truth is not what my mood inclines me
  to understand,
    to agree with --
Life modifies my
  criteria of truth.

Going on and on,
  past present vision,
    toward the dim of future unknown . . . .
To perhaps overturn what's enjoyed right now,
  what's desired;
    but is it desirable?

Who knows, but who knows better than you --
  about trying, not fearing destruction.
For the soul oversees -- seeing only the Real:
  what the 'I' would love to believe.

Time

It is a day like no other --
Time sees to that.

Only the mind mistakes it
For yesterday,
Or tomorrow.

Pathways

The balance between willing, self-directing --
And letting, allowing the moment to bud,
To unflower,
To fertilize the fields of our existence . . . .

Existing for the orchid, the berry,
The morning of harvest,
The golden-grained eve . . . .

The color, the sound,
The scent of the people,
Their seeds of hope, ready for soil . . . .

For their coming to the time
To plant, implant,
To be water, and warmth, and awareness . . . .

To push up the seed,
To step out and grow,
The stem and the stalk
To the sky . . . .

Peace-time yearning, learning --
Holding open the door to the heart:
    It's a rainbow!

Once Again

From the cozy comfort of a fire-warmed bed,
   I watched the morning say hello --
The sunrise:
     heralded by pink and orange glows
        on the clouds of dawn,
Illuminating the frosted fields of grasses
     that had become white crystal fingers overnight,
        branches of lacy ice and winter dignity.

The cedar outside took note,
     and in beauty's silent words
     gave a welcoming nod.

Where depression goes
     before such an augur of good
        is nature's secret --
But errant thoughts are clearly banished
     somewhere far removed
        from the world of newborn light,
        and newfound hope.

The Ferry

I stand on the 5 a.m. deck,
Not more than a yard or two from the sea,
At a bow that ploughs through wind & wave,
No rail to bar the scene.

The freshness of scent
From forest-green mountains,
Sea-swept and sweet with dew,
Silver-peach tint of ripple-skin waters,
Sky a pale, silky hue.

With sparkle-white Venus & red-sparked Mars,
A thin, blue dot of Saturn,
Mercury dim in the mist-orange haze,
By rock cliffs young, unweathered.

Dark bird lifts and gliding, coasts,
Encircling the pre-morning sky,
Geography changing, layers of land
Shifting place as the ferry goes by.

And I'm lost in a reverie,
Found in a dream,
A place where the heart can soar,
Free where the will can wander,
Unchained,
In the lap of a breath-new dawn.

The Magic Potion

O, your presence --
A capsule of it would sweeten me
    like essence of rose,
    like red of wine,
    like waiting lips,
      my love.

In Season

Your kisses:
    the buds
    for an April disposition.

The Feeling is Mutual

Press me to you gently:
Fur on field,
Wave on wind,
Silk on stream,
Pearl on petal.

Press me like a leaf
On a sheaf of poems,
A lock of hair
On the chest
Of a loving, perfect lover.

Message

It was not until dew-time,
When beads of light made necklaces
Out of spiders' webs,
And every leaf had its own jeweled drop
That became a mirror or a rainbow
When pierced by the golden sun . . . .

It was not until the wakening of the land,
Mist rising, birds opening their wings --

That she found out her lover was coming,
And soon:
Oh, morning of hearts,
Rejoice!

Seeing Is Believing

She lifts her head, and gazes:
    stars of golden fire,
    stars of diamond clarity --
The night's tiara of jewels.

She moves an eye,
And perspective shows moon,
    peaks,
    trees,
    a man's silhouette --
The man who sits beside her.

It's a love and a life of charm;
A mood and a faithful feeling.
The dove defies the storm,
And like the flower,
Finds the light.

The Caution

Projection:
You see him with false perfection,
Leading later,
Of course,
To rejection,
Dejection.

The cure:
A good dose of discretion!

Definitions of Love

1.

It's a game that's won
When none oppose
And all know how to score.

2.

Who needs to speak
When love envelopes
And seals us with a kiss?

3.

Mink rubs ermine softly;
Pair of wings in soaring;
Fish in league with water,
Neither struggling to part.

4.

Entirely attired,
Bedecked, unfurled
In beauty's flush-cheeked hue --
This fashion's always
Currently in style.

5.

In you come to bed,
Lamb-like, nuzzling.

A Love Primer

A bond that shimmers with laughing delight,
And shivers with zesty desire,
Silvering our circling lives with the light
Of a moon on the frosty river.

Doing for each other what the sun and the rain
Gladly do for the leaves,
And the summer --

The way we relate is the only way:
To dance the dance of one's self,
In hand with another.

Hymn

The eloquence of night
    lay like a finger
        upon her lips --
Hushing quietly the words
    before they could form.

Serenity's crescent hung above,
    a golden scarf of moon;
As she gazed inwardly,
    toward
        the centerpoint.

Encompassed by the clearest water
    curved by an ancient urn,
Yearning for the breath
    of vivid sight --

She softly sang:
'Twas the song
    of the silent voice
        that made her strong.

Credo

Infinite is the capacity
To think, to feel, to leap --
Winsome as a fawn,
Thundrous as a waterfall.

And in early morning eyes
Lying dreamily by your side,
In stars of softness pouring skies of light,
In mountain skies,
Blue and full with nature's own forgiveness --

In all the presents wrapped with divinity's ribbons,
I believe.

Transformation

The moon of the wind allures,
The dawning clouds of light are dancing . . . .

And tears of bitter past
Become the dew upon the rose.

The Knack

Access to the inner worlds,
The heart-warm turns of mind --

And laughing with the suns and streams,
The textured earth eternal.

The Love Garden

In a bed of bright & juicy green,
Stalks & stems of chlorophyll and silence,
I lie, intoned
In the sunlight of the day --

No impositions;
No thrusting of mind
On the presence,
The essence,
Nature's own ways . . . .

The warm breeze speaks,
The star-flowers answer,
And a chorus of grass-blades
Swaying in waves --

Their thin, fine hairs of silvery gold
Reflective,
        meditative,
                precise --
The infinitely small
Containing the infinitely great.

The Search

In the labyrinths,
Encoded places
    where pathways are hard to unwind,

In the intricacies
That lead us through
    the revolving doors of the mind,

In the words that perplex,
In sands that blow
    obscurity in our eyes --

We meet our small defeats:
And yet, the hope of freedom's find.

Graced

Now the balance is complete,
The line of time perfected;
Naturalness being the skin of a peach,
Fruit-flesh juicy,
And close,
And kind,
Satin ruminations:
A pinkish shine
On a vine of ancient gold.

The Nurturing

Dappled hills,
Dipping/rising folds of green,
Liquid drops of sunlight stream
From an early rising sun.

Shamelessly,
The grass drinks in
The golden, sailing snowflakes;
As a child,
Yet to be born,
Waits in the womb, warmed unknowingly.

A simple acceptance,
Receiving from an unseen,
Trusted source:

Thus we, like the babe,
The grass and the sky,
But dimly perceive
The place
From which Love grows.

Cherry Picking

Like a mother feeding her babe,
  lovingly and caringly,
The cherry tree dangled her blushed, clustered fruits
    for our fingers and palms to tug, retrieve
    from between the leaves and branches.

We climbed on skyward ladders,
  raindrops dripping through shapes of green,
Reaching, arms outstretched,
  for the shining offering.
The birds had already begun their nibbles,
    but we creatures of earth had plenty left
    to feast upon, acknowledge,
    and thanks-in-our hearts collect . . . .
Appreciating the way Nature very simply
    and very beautifully
    grants a wish, a promise, a privilege
      to her children.

The rotund, good-natured Italian grocer,
    owner of the tree,
    helped us out whenever he could --
Placing the ladder, proffering advice,
    even perching his portly body top-step
    to reach the branches beyond.

That night, lit by kerosene lamplight,
   the spheres of red and white rested in a mound
   in a large, round silvery bowl.

Morsels of sweetness upon our tongues,
We heated jars for the canning,
   for winter treats
   of pies, preserves, desserts.

May we learn to return to earth
All the gifts she so willingly gives.

The Wish

Give me liberty,
And give me breadth,
Give me light,
And give me depth.

Agony is worth a word,
But ecstacy much more --
Sweep me like the winds
Through heaven's door.

Water Music

By and by, river walk:
I know by the sounds of the chiming --
Layers of waves
Swept up in the arms of an ear
That yearns -- and listens.

The Dream

We are the green of emeralds,
    grecian gold,
    a hallowed refrain of opals . . . .
Minaret eyes,
    silver-sword minds,
    piercing the veiled horizon.

Lemon, orange, violet, blue,
    a multi-faceted crystal,
Gems and tints,
    waterfall glints --

The secret:
    To be open --
    And receive.

These, We Treasure

These are the times
When the vividness so surrounds me,
Not merely hinting at, but actualizing
What is genuine and real:
  colors, forms, scents, silhouettes,
  sounds & auras,
  truths . . . .

When my world is so complete
There is no crack for winds unsure,
For sighs to enter . . . .

When enduring and transience
  are closest of friends,
And time a liquid unhurrying . . . .

When the sea is my mentor,
Its rhythms a heart,
An insistent, flowing bloodbeat . . . .

When the forest silence sings,
When every flicker burns,
When even black of night knows how to play
  the game of magic. . . .

When solitude's full as a family hearth,
  and company as comfortable as one's self . . . .

When growth and death and all the cycles --
  all plenitude and scarcity,
  and the seeking inbetween --
Are equally drawn and blessed . . . .

When purposes vast with promise
  suggest a meaning to it all . . . .

These are the times:
  moment-precious as the dawn.

Must Be Heaven

Chance and free-wheeling spirit:
The song clears a path,
The beckoning wave of a banner,
A worry-free glance --

As motion by motion,
Note by note,
I tune up the strings of my heart,
Celestial music circling in space:
The lyrics of dancing stars.

Knowing How to Grow

Mind —
The mirror of experience,
The sifter and shaper of memory,
Of thoughts culled from the ways we perceive,
The ways we believe,
The ways our hearts persuade . . . .

Mind —
Feeling what we've gleaned, dreamed,
In the night & mystery caverns . . . .

And yet we remain as naked as babes
After years of clothing with concepts --

For we're always new-born,
New-clothed and fed,
At the hands of Fate & Fortune.

That's the Way

Arnie says,
"Suffering comes with life. It's whether
We want to learn from it."

Dean asks,
"But why do we have to go through the same lessons
Over and over?"

Arnie:
"It's like a blacksmith forging metal --
He keeps firing and pounding it,
And each time it gets stronger.
Life is like that --
You keep going through the experiences,
And keep getting stronger.
And the people who don't seem to suffer,
Who have money or fame or worldly success --
They still have the karma of living in their body,
And they aren't too happy
If they have to screw other people
To get where they are."

"If a person's senses are refined,"
He continues,
"You're going to suffer a lot --
Suffer other people's suffering . . . .

But you experience a lot of profound things, too:
That door opens up,
You're touched,
You can appreciate beauty.

The people who are callous
Just go through life
Not experiencing the deepness --
And that is punishment in itself."

For on earth,
Under sky,
The way shall be revealed.

Two Worlds

Beneath roses,
Earth.
Beneath freedom,
Body pronounces its shape & form.

We can <u>be</u> both,
    <u>do</u> both,
    <u>have</u> both:
If ether and rock unite.

Like a bubble of air in a hand-blown glass --
Not trapped,
But forever open,
    forever becoming.

Day of Birth

Life arcs, sweeps, soars
    like a bird of fall color --
Reds, golds, oranges leaping . . . .

And in its midst,
    like a wind on a rushing wing,
    arms wide,
        I fly.

How the glitter reflects in my eye!
How the melody tickles my mind !

Drenched with the suns & the moons & the rains,
    I have found a home-like nest
    in the heart of the sky.

Flight

The bird whose wings are turquoise, long,
   bejeweled with nature's diamonds --
Sweeps and gives its ermine ease,
   without thought,
      to the blue-arrowed sky.

The Prayer

The yearning --
   and then,
      the contentment;
The seeking, the relishing --
   and then,
      the response;
The poignant request --
   and then,
      the fulfillment:
Return,
   heart-felt,
      for the Asking.

The Link

Why is love always mythically-dimensioned,
Apollo embracing Aphrodite ever again?

Why are Man and Woman the genesis
Of logos and pathos,
Eros and passion without end?

Each dip in the cup of twoness
Brings forth trumpets, thunders,
The grandest stellar procession;
Each wave of the wand,
A tale of prince and princess.

As the fullness moon never ceases to awe,
Silver of face, space-haunted;
And the tiniest tremblings of lacquer-blue seas
Never cease to intrigue the sands . . . .

So a glance of eyes, a brush of arms,
A scent of breath upon breath,
Never cease to throw a cape of Light
'Round the coupling together of hearts.

One

Like leaves overlapping,
Afloat,
Creek-pulled in drift,
Water-held,
Wind-bonded --

He, and I:
In the stream of a gentle love.

No Dialogue Completer

I kiss my love;
He answers
With a smile.

The Overture

Born in an Eden of dreams,
Born to the song
Of your whispers,
Born like a silk-pink petal of skin:

To lay soft in the winds
Of your spring.

Movement Piece

Living in the spirit,
  no finality --
A secret, bangled waltz
  around the lake and islet moon.

(These thoughts as clouds go rafting by,
  from gray to whisper pink,
  and dim-lit eve enfolds
  the curving hills . . .)

Inexplicable,
  this mystery tour,
Life's tunnels, shifting seas,
On and on and on toward inner knowing.

How lastingness
  is emerging,
    and growth through changeless being . . . .
Singing my way to fathom stars,
  and lily hearts,
    and deep blue nights --
And all the candy loves
  and tragic moments . . . .

And out of shifting voices,
    spoken reason,
    passion's feeling --

The baskets of cherries I kissed,
    knowing the honey & the rose combined . . . .

It all comes through,
    it all comes flowering through.

In recognition
    of all
    that's come before;
In recognition
    of all
    to come my way --

In the way I'm lifted down
    from sky to earth,
And once more toward
    courageous heaven --

I tip my hat,
    my glass will tinkle too,
    in toast: To Life!

Option

Subjectively,
Perspectively,
The picture is never quite clear.
Mood-glasses color,
A fog of inner emotions
Obscures the view.

And yet,
If we'd make every effort to see
With eyes not cast down,
But up --
We'd progress to a clearer line of sight:
By the light
Of our very own moon.

To Carry Me On

Let the enthusiasm of the worlds,
Elated places where stars beknight the trees,
And rivers are leaping --
Let these become my home.

And when I am far away,
When joy is a distant geography of memory --
Let the scent of those realms waft gently,
Encircle my nostrils with hints
Of peach-flame tints & tones.

And when I am so lost,
That even thoughts of the dream
Are uncapturable;
When comforts of past and future
Dissolve in the dim and grim absurd --

What salvation can I gain?

Serenity.
Let calmness prevail,
Let peace pervade the heart.

An Angel's Grace

Love opened the gate,
Love enveloped us --

Love plunked us in her cup of warm honey,
Suspended us in space;

Love gave, and we were ready to be
        the gift,
        the giving,
        the given.

Up and Away

Crystalline, glass-blown, starry leaves
Of night;
Listening -- their aura is an echo.

Flute combs its way into my bones,
My mouth, my mind;
A choral fugue, curtain of lifting dawn.

More of "yes" means less of loss,
Those blind & sightless imperatives --
Pressured vices,
Vises that crush the juice --
But do not pour forth.

For soon is not too soon;
Enough is not too much.
Filling up, nectar-plucked,
A wreath around my shoulders.

And so I dream, I think, I wink the way
And glide the night . . . .
A smooth-fingered feel,
With sash & satin finish . . . .
And rest myself when the time is ripe
Upon a log-of-rhythm --
I've learned my lesson:
Make hay while the fun still shines.

Progress / Process

Make my stance
Like that of a noble tree . . . .

Standing,

Yet growing,

Firm and stable,

Yet able

To bend with the breeze.

The Good, The True, The Beautiful

Intimate connection,
　　Life's refined reflection,
　　　Soul's intense perfection:
Plato's trilogy of truth.

The Appreciation

How like a shadow,
   but dimly distinguished
   from the downcast eyes
      of a pale and early dawn,
Do we pass from one phase of life to another!

Subtleties take us by the hand,
And lead us on.

We cross the stepping-stones
By movements unnoticed,
   motions undetected --
Yet here we are found,
At another place & time.

To witness these events,
We'd need to climb to the vantage-point
Of a God.

But from our own near altar,
Unknowing how these & all miracles are created,
We can only whisper words of wonder --
And prepare for our new abode.

The Visit

Exploring realities under the arched chapel
Of our ideas,
Encircling worlds by words,
Forms by imaged conceptions --
We view the moon,
Yellow misted,
Framed by ebony, bronze-beige, blue.

Inside the cabin of wood in the woods,
She sings, sweet-voiced, soprano --
A pearl in the heart of a flower, hymnal --
The peaced sound of silence beyond.

Gray cat approaches, a still, quiet sculpture,
Curving, furred tail of grace . . . .
Making a toast with clink of hot mugs:
"To a future we know not of."

Conversing with heart,
Science fact, science fiction,
Tales and musings without number . . . .
Formed by the trees, the night wind, and notions
Of time --
And the song of the timeless.

Silhouettes, flames, gleams of whim,
Fires of shining purpose . . . .
Partnered, voyaging sails
Blown by the winds of imagination.

And our souls unfold in mysterious balance,
Like the sun and the moon,
Both sides:
The "I" of the self,
The name that we know --

And a deep-rooted faith in the All.

Image

Maybe it's all in the flowerbud,
The bloom that begins its own miracle --

    opens,
        petals,
            shows,

Unabashedly.

Peaked

Living within the skin
Of silvered existence --

Hear the cat-like walk of the stars,
Feel the pulse of rains,
The manes of mountain stallions . . . .

I in the round of the moon's soprano,
I in the wake of the night,
I in the echo of amber-gaze eyes,
I in the lake of your fire.

Toward the New

The possibles reach out with all honesty, all fluidity,
    all stretchings of the fabric of being,
Making their way past blocks, rocks,
    walls of stone, silly excuses --

Past tables of seated refusers,
Underneath curtains rung down
    and tin roofs hiding the stars . . . .

And they gain their entrance,
Fences or not,
And sneak inside our yards --
Proceeding to deal us the wildest cards:
    a deck that's stacked to woo us,
        however unwilling,
        to their game.

But if we resist, dare not respond,
Pretend we can't be what they tell us we may;
Shrivel our eyes and sink our fears
    where hope and strength should anchor --

The ostrich stance will get us what Death will bring:
    only that much sooner.

To accept the challenge of the new,
    the unknown,
      the aches & ecstacies of growing!

To keep the appetite acute, not sated
    with meals of the past,
      those old-hat harvests --
Ghosts of ideas, phantoms of joy,
    mere memories of truths.

This is the mysterious call,
This, the colored ball we're tossed,
The imperative chance:
      To go dancing,
      Yes, dancing,
      With life!

Reality

Worlds of flowers do not pretend,
Worlds of flowers do not defend --

They reap the wind,
Their suns write lilies:

And to christen with scent is their dream.

Out of Bounds

"What is possible,"
   said the turtle,
   speaking to the wind,
"Is everything within my shell --
   tho I know not what's without."

"What is actual,"
   answered the wind,
   with a gentle wave of the hand,
"Is you becoming
   everything you ask."

The Harkening

Dream believer --
Does the incense swirl,
A paisley grace,
A beat of the sea-weave breathing,
Forests grazing green on blue,
The trees and heavens yearning . . . .

Listening to drums of the winds and sun,
The rhythms of star and river,
The yellow just peeking at winter's end --
The seeds call out for sowing.

Melody

The violet-lemon tinge on the mountain,
Sunrise soft as a fawn:
Eucalyptus, fragrance,
Dew-sniff air,
The robe of renewal: dawn.

Saber-swift jumps over obstacles, barriers,
Humps of immovable stone --
Dark-hovering boulders
Appearing mid-stream,
Barring the way towards home.

Sky-waving treetops are signals of wind,
And birds with their high-pealed calls,
Vast, moving canopies of golden white clouds,
Visits of traveling stars.

The favors like tumbleweeds
Blow 'cross our paths,
The air sings and whispers the way:
A deep-throated, silver-sweet flute in the night,
And a violin song in the day.

Full Moon / Silver Glimpses

Here the moon collided with our yes;
Here the moon made us gasp,
    and wonder,
        and trust --

Believe once again
    in the fairy dust,
        the sparkle-star light
      of the night:

    Unveiled, Alive.

About the Author

Gloria's first "book" of poetry appeared in grade school -- loose-leaf pages stapled between construction paper covers, in which she wrote, "The moon is cuddled by a blue blanket of sky . . . ."

She's been moon-gazing ever since, literally as well as metaphorically. The quest for love, beauty and truth took her from Brooklyn to becoming a philosophy major at Barnard College ('67); from the woods of Oregon to the oceanside at Isla Vista, California; from a cabin on the west coast of British Columbia, Canada, to San Francisco.

Two volumes of poetry emerged along the way, which she produced under her own imprint, Little Wing Publishing -- <u>POEMS OF SONG & PASSION</u> (1975), and <u>LOVEBUD: EXPECTATIONS OF THE HEART</u> (1978). There have also been feature articles and essays printed in newspapers and magazines, a number of nonfiction books rewritten/ revised as a free-lance editor, and two works of fiction (as yet unpublished): a series of satirical short stories, and a fantasy novel.

Gloria had early encouragement from her parents in playing the piano and drawing, as well as great training from her two brothers and two sisters in laughing and loving -- all of which she still enjoys; along with constantly being surprised by life!

INDEX TO TITLES

202.